The NEW Putting on the BRAKES

UNDERSTANDING AND TAKING CONTROL OF YOUR ADD OR ADHD

SECOND EDITION

by Patricia O. Quinn, M.D. and Judith M. Stern, M.A.

illustrated by Joe Lee

MAGINATION PRESS ✸ WASHINGTON D.C.
American Psychological Association

For Uzi, Talia, and Naomi — JMS

For all the kids with AD/HD. "Keep smiling.
It makes everyone wonder what you're up to ~ Anonymous" — POQ

My sincerest thanks and love to my son Brandon
who has taught me a great deal about AD/HD — JL

Published by
MAGINATION PRESS
An Educational Publishing Foundation Book
American Psychological Association
750 First Street, NE
Washington, DC 20002

For more information about our books, including a complete catalog,
please write to us, call 1-800-374-2721, or visit our website at www.maginationpress.com.

Editor: Becky Shaw
Art Director: Susan K. White
Printed by Worzalla, Stephens Point, Wisconsin

Library of Congress Cataloging-in-Publication Data

Quinn, Patricia O.
Putting on the brakes : understanding and taking control of your ADD or ADHD /
by Patricia O. Quinn and Judith M. Stern ; illustrated by Joe Lee. — 2nd ed.
p. cm.
ISBN-13: 978-1-4338-0386-4 (hardcover : alk. paper)
ISBN-10: 1-4338-0386-0 (hardcover : alk. paper)
ISBN-13: 978-1-4338-0387-1 (pbk. : alk. paper)
ISBN-10: 1-4338-0387-9 (pbk. : alk. paper) 1. Attention-deficit hyperactivity
disorder—Juvenile literature. I. Stern, Judith M. II. Lee, Joe, 1953- III. Title.
RJ506.H9Q5482 2009
618.92'8589—dc22   2008017581

10 9 8 7 6 5 4 3 2 1

CONTENTS

FOREWORD
To Parents and Professionals

When young people learn they have an attention disorder (ADD or ADHD), they have many questions, doubts, and fears. This book, written by a pediatrician and an educator, addresses children's needs and questions. School-age children respect material they find in a book, especially when it confirms or expands what they have learned from their own experience or an adult they respect. Children need reassurance that the problems they have are not unique to them. They benefit from a sense that help is available and that they themselves can be a powerful force in their own treatment.

Over the years, we have heard from children, parents and professionals about how *Putting on the Brakes* has helped children learn more about themselves and find good ways to cope with AD/HD. This new edition of *Putting on the Brakes* attempts to give children with ADD and ADHD a sense of control and a perception of obtainable goals. It includes the significant advances that have been made in the treatment and understanding of ADD and ADHD since the publication of the first edition 16 years ago. The book is written in language that children can understand, providing realistic information that can be used in their daily lives.

The new edition contains updated information on AD/HD, including a look at the many important developments that have occurred since *Putting on the Brakes* was first written. Children, parents and professionals will benefit from the fact that, over the years, a great deal more has been learned about how to successfully manage this disorder. Our aim was to share these new developments, along with information from the earlier edition,

using concepts and vocabulary appropriate to the young reader. We have also expanded the book to include more ideas and techniques for children to use to help themselves. New chapters have been included in order to share many of the new approaches to dealing with AD/HD. A special emphasis has been placed on empowering young people to take control, rather than feel disadvantaged.

The book was designed to be used with young people between the ages of 8 and 13. By reading the book together with their children, parents may begin an ongoing discussion that will provide information and reassurance. It is important to keep the hopeful message of this book in mind while reading and talking together with children. Depending on reading ability, the book may be read by the child alone or out loud by an adult. Efforts have been made to explain unfamiliar or difficult words. A glossary has been provided at the back of the book so that the reader may conveniently look up unfamiliar words as often as necessary.

In this book, we have chosen to use the terminology AD/HD when discussing attention deficit disorders with and without hyperactivity. This book is meant to be used by children with ADD or ADHD, as the explanations and coping strategies are relevant to both populations. To minimize confusion, we will refer to AD/HD to include both disorders.

In order to avoid overwhelming the child with too much information all at once, it is recommended that the book be read and discussed in sections. By providing frequent opportunities to discuss the contents of the book, an adult can help a child manage what is being covered. These discussions can be used to correct misunderstandings, share personal insights, or raise further questions.

Children should be encouraged to read the book a number of times, as they may absorb additional meaning each time. The book might also be shared with siblings and friends, with the guidance of an informed adult. This book is not meant to replace professional consultation and treatments, which should be part of an ongoing process in the lives of children diagnosed with AD/HD.

Teachers, counselors, and psychologists may find this book and its companion activity books (*The "Putting on the Brakes" Activity Book for Kids* and *50 Activities and Games for Kids with ADHD*) useful in helping children better understand AD/HD and its impact on their lives. These books may also be used by professionals when working with a small group of children who are engaged in the process of learning about their attention disorder.

Understanding AD/HD is not an easy task. However, beginning the process will open children and their parents to a world of positive possibilities.

— Patricia O. Quinn, M.D.
— Judith M. Stern, M.A.

PART 1

Understanding AD/HD

AD/HD: What Is It?

How Do You Know If You Have ADD or ADHD?

Who Can Have AD/HD?

What Is Going on in the AD/HD Brain?

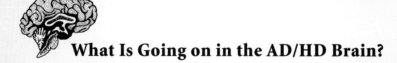

How Does AD/HD Make You Feel?

CHAPTER 1

AD/HD: What Is It?

Imagine a sleek, red sports car driving around a track. It's flying down the stretches, speeding around the curves, smooth and low to the road, the engine racing…BUT… it has no brakes. It can't stop when the driver wants it to stop. It can't slow down to a safer speed. It may get off the track or even crash! It will certainly have a hard time proving to everyone what it really can do.

If you have an attention deficit disorder, you may be like that racing car. You have a good engine (with lots of thinking power) and a good strong body, but your brakes don't work very well. You might not be able to keep still, stay focused or stop yourself from doing something, even when you know you should.

What Is AD/HD?

Not everyone with an attention disorder is exactly the same. A person with AD/HD may have any or all of the following problems:

Trouble paying attention

Trouble focusing on just one thing at a time

Trouble keeping still

Trouble thinking before acting

Trouble keeping track of things

Trouble learning in school

Experts who work with kids with attention disorders have names for different types of AD/HD, depending on which problems are causing the most trouble. That is why some kids have ADD while others have ADHD. They simply have different problems.

⊛ One type of attention disorder (**Inattentive Type**) describes kids who mainly have difficulty paying attention (*inattention*) and staying focused (*distractibility*).

⊛ Another type (**Hyperactive/Impulsive Type**) includes kids who have more difficulty with keeping still when they need to (*hyperactivity*) and who frequently act before they think things through (*impulsivity*).

⊛ And finally, many kids with attention disorders have a combination of all of these problems and, therefore, they have a third type of AD/HD that has been called **Combined Type**.

You have probably seen and heard different names and initials used to describe these different types of attention problems. ADD, ADHD, and AD/HD are the most common names used. In this book, we will usually use the term AD/HD to include all of the types. No matter which of the types describes you, this book will help you better understand and take control of your ADD or ADHD.

The following pages describe in more detail some of the problems that young people with AD/HD may face. As you are reading, see if any of these problems sound familiar to you.

Inattention *(Trouble Paying Attention)*

If you have trouble staying tuned in or paying attention to any one thing for more than a few minutes, you may have a short attention span. If you only have problems in this area and are not hyperactive, you just have attention deficits (ADD). This is where the first part of the name AD/HD comes from: attention deficit hyperactivity disorder. A deficit means that there is less of something than is needed.

Having difficulty paying attention affects many things. Problems with attention may result in your taking longer to start or finish assignments. At home or school, if you are not paying close attention when someone is giving directions, you may not know what you should be doing. When talking with others or during class discussion, trouble paying attention may cause you to lose track of what is being said and result in your feeling confused or frustrated.

We all find it easier to **concentrate** when we are interested in something, so paying attention may not be a problem when you are doing something that you like. You may find it much easier to pay attention when the subject interests you, but feel quite lost when the topic is difficult or uninteresting. Your parents and teachers may be confused by this and think you should be able to pay attention all the time. You may need to make them aware of the difficulties you are having and let them know when it is difficult for you to concentrate.

You may get angry when an adult keeps telling you to pay attention, especially when you feel that you are trying very hard to do just that. And in spite of your efforts, the results may not be as good as you (or your parents or teachers) wish.

Distractibility *(Trouble Focusing on Just One Thing)*

Kids with AD/HD have more trouble than others focusing on just one thing. Unrelated thoughts, ideas, sights, and sounds keep interrupting their train of thought.

When you are taking a math test, thoughts about a ball game, lunch, or other activities may interfere and keep you from concentrating on the test. It may be hard to listen to your teacher when you find so many other things to look at or listen to in the classroom. You may be playing with the pencil on your desk or watching the man mowing the lawn outside instead of focusing on the lesson. A bird singing outside the window or someone walking near you may keep you from hearing the teacher give a homework assignment.

Kids say that having AD/HD feels like constantly switching channels on a TV. Their brains are just not able to stay tuned in to one channel. Because of this difficulty staying focused, you

sometimes miss what is going on around you. When many different thoughts keep popping into your head, one right after the other, they interfere with what you are trying to do.

Hyperactivity
(Trouble Keeping Still)

If you are hyperactive, it may be difficult for you to keep still. You feel like you always have to be moving. Sitting in one place is especially hard and may make you feel very restless. You feel that you have to stand up, fidget, or move around. Not being able to move may make you feel upset, anxious, tired, or sleepy. Some hyperactive kids may also tend to talk all the time without giving other people a turn.

It is frustrating to be told over and over to stop moving or to sit still. Like the race car that doesn't have any brakes, you may have difficulty stopping even when you want to stop.

Impulsivity *(Trouble Thinking Before Acting)*

Sometimes you may do or say things without thinking. You may ride your bicycle through your parents' garden, or call out the answer in class without raising your hand, or start a test before all the directions are given. You may interrupt others or say the first thing that comes into your head, whatever that is!

Doing or saying something without thinking—with no brakes to stop you — is called impulsive behavior.

People may ask, "Why did you do that?" At that moment, you may not know why, so you'll say, "I don't know." After some thought, you may be able to discuss what you did wrong. However, you may still forget to "think before you act" the next time. This can be very frustrating for both you and the people around you.

Disorganization *(Trouble Keeping Track of Things)*

Kids with AD/HD can be disorganized. Keeping track of belongings, school assignments, **due dates** or chores may be a big problem. You may forget or lose things more than other people do. You may not know how to keep track of time or how to manage it well. In the morning, you may suddenly discover you have run out of time. The school bus has arrived, and you are still not ready. You may forget homework assignments or not have the correct books at home to complete an assignment. As a result, you may not hand your homework in on time. Or you may postpone school assignments until the last minute and then have to rush. The work you turn in may not show all you really know. You might have done better if you had started earlier. You may then feel disappointed when you get your assignment back with many corrections, knowing that you could have done better.

Learning Difficulties *(Trouble Learning in School)*

Because of all these problems, kids with AD/HD may have trouble in school. Sometimes it is more difficult to do reading and writing assignments, or learn math as easily as other students seem to be able to do. If this sounds like you, you may need extra help with learning. You are just as smart as other kids, but you may need a tutor or a coach to keep you organized or to help you with your work.

Some kids with AD/HD may also have a **learning disability** in a specific subject area, such as reading, math, or writing. This means that they are learning, but at a level that is below what is expected for their intelligence and grade level. You could have a learning disability in one subject, and do very well in other school subjects. Or you may have difficulties in several subjects. When these difficulties are combined with AD/HD, school may sometimes feel especially hard. If a child with AD/HD also has a learning disability, he or she may work with a **learning specialist** or **tutor** to make progress in the subject or subjects that are causing trouble. Because teachers now know many good ways to work with students who have learning problems, schools can give extra support so that these students can do a better job and get better grades in their classes.

Most kids with AD/HD have lots of questions.

Why can I pay attention better on certain days?

Am I the only one with this problem?

How do I know if I have ADD or ADHD?

Is there something wrong with my brain?

Why am I like this?

In this book, we will try to answer your questions.

CHAPTER 2

How Do You Know If You Have ADD or ADHD?

Everyone has some of the problems we have talked about in the last chapter, some of the time. It can be hard to pay attention in school when you are thinking about your upcoming birthday party or your new baby sister. If you're going through a tough time at home, like your parents are getting a divorce or a loved one has recently died, worry or sadness

may make you restless, **irritable**, or forgetful, or have trouble paying attention. However, if you have had attention problems for a long time and they are not related to a stressful situation, you may have ADD or ADHD. Deciding if you have ADD or ADHD can be done only by **professionals** who are experts in this area. These experts may include **pediatricians, psychologists, psychiatrists**, and **neurologists**—different kinds of doctors who know all about ADHD and can help kids who have it.

To determine if you have ADD or ADHD, you may be seen by a doctor, **counselor**, or psychologist. Sometimes you need to visit more than one specialist. During these visits, these specialists test how you learn and your ability to concentrate. The testing may take several hours. These experts will also talk to your parents and teachers. They might ask your teachers and parents to fill out forms that describe your behavior, attention, and learning ability. After gathering all this information, the experts can then come to a decision about whether or not you have ADD (attention deficit disorder) or ADHD (attention deficit hyperactivity disorder).

CHAPTER 3

Who Can Have AD/HD?

Can you guess who in this class has ADD or ADHD? You can't tell, because kids with AD/HD look just like everybody else!

About one in every 15 to 20 kids has a problem with attention that affects their learning or behavior. As many as 4.4 million school-age kids in the United States are thought to have ADD or ADHD. A class of 20 might have one or two kids with some form of AD/HD, and both boys and girls can have ADD or ADHD. We also know that kids all around the world have AD/HD. Did you know that the earlier edition of this book that you are now reading has been translated into many other languages, so that AD/HD kids from around the world can learn about themselves, too?

You may not be able to point out kids with AD/HD very easily, because they look just like everybody else. People used to think that kids with AD/HD were easy to spot because of their hyperactivity. But we now know that many kids have ADD and are not hyperactive, so they may be more difficult to identify.

Although you may feel a little different from the other kids in your class who do not have difficulties with attention, you have lots of company when you consider how many other kids your age have AD/HD!

AD/HD in Boys and Girls

Some people think that only boys have ADD or ADHD. Wrong! This is simply not true. Girls can have AD/HD, too. Both boys and girls with AD/HD may have trouble sitting still and they may fidget a lot. However, girls with AD/HD usually have more problems with attention than hyperactivity. When hyperactivity is present in girls, it might show up as lots of talking or as out-of-control emotions. Whatever their symptoms, girls with AD/HD have just as many problems at school and at home as boys with AD/HD.

AD/HD in Your Family

AD/HD can be **inherited**, so you might find that there are other people in your family with the same or similar problems. If this happens, you might want to talk to some of these relatives about your AD/HD, because they may have a good understanding of how you feel.

CHAPTER 4

What Is Going on in the AD/HD Brain?

The brain is made up of several areas, each with its own specific job. The outside layers of the brain are called the **cerebral cortex**. This is the part of the brain where most thinking and learning takes place. It is also where memories are stored.

Under the cortex is an area called the **subcortex**. The subcortex helps you stay alert and coordinates your brain's activities. It contains the **relay system**, which has many jobs. The relay system takes information coming in from your senses (like hearing, sight, touch) and decides where it should go in the cortex. It tells you what to pay attention to at the time, and sends messages to "turn on" other parts of your brain, including the braking or inhibiting system. The center for your emotions (anger, fear, happiness or excitement) and the reward center (an area that becomes active when something gives you pleasure or makes you happy) are also in this layer. That probably explains why you can pay better attention when you like a certain activity or when you know you will receive a reward when you are finished.

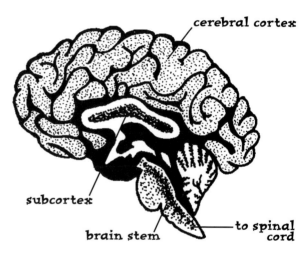

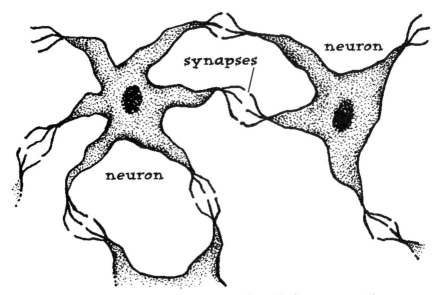

The brain is made up of many cells called **neurons**. These cells work together, but do not actually touch each other. They are separated by a tiny space called a **synapse**. The neurons send information or messages to each other by sending a chemical messenger across this space. These messengers are called **neurotransmitters**.

For the neuron to relay the message to the cells around it, there must be enough of the neurotransmitter (*messenger*) to do the job, and the messenger must stay in the synapse (*space*) long enough to join with a receptor on each of the surrounding cells. This joining of the neurotransmitter to the **receptor** is like a key fitting into a lock. When the neurotransmitter (working like a key) fits into the receptor (working like a lock), it opens the door for messages to get through.

When the brain is working properly, there is enough neurotransmitter to turn on the cells and deliver the messages where they are supposed to go. In the brain of a person with ADD or ADHD, this may not always be happening. Messages to put on the brakes, to slow down, and to pay attention may not be getting through effectively. A person may then act without thinking (*impulsivity*) or be very distracted by other things (*distractability*).

Scientists have several explanations for why the messages are poorly transmitted (*sent*) when someone has AD/HD. When scientists took **scans** (*pictures*) of the brain in people with AD/HD, they found that the areas that control attention and help with planning ahead are not working properly or have developed more slowly. When this happens there is not enough of the neurotransmitter to turn on the neurons in these areas and keep them turned on so that they can do their job.

Scientists have also found that there is a system in each cell that takes the neurotransmitter from the synapse (*space*) and carries it back inside the neuron (*cell*) that first sent it out. This is called the **transporter system**. It seems that some people with AD/HD have too many of these transporters (*proteins*). This causes the neurotransmitter to be taken back into the cell before it can relay the message to nearby cells. When this happens, other areas of the brain cannot do their job. This may help explain why kids with AD/HD have trouble paying attention or getting organized. It helps explain why they may forget or lose things, or act as if they have no brakes.

Scientists also know that while these problems with the neurotransmitters affect some of the brain's jobs, like learning and remembering, they do not affect intelligence, personality, or creativity. Kids with AD/HD are just as smart, talented, and healthy as other kids.

CHAPTER 5

How Does AD/HD Make You Feel?

ids with ADD or ADHD have lots of different thoughts and feelings. Sometimes you feel:

Confused   *Impatient*   *Dumb*

Overloaded   *Restless*

Scared   *Angry*   *Frustrated*

Misunderstood   *Teased*

Tense   *Anxious*   *Picked on*

Unpopular      *Lost*

Forgetful

Let's look at some of the causes of these feelings:

✳ You may feel confused or lost if you tune out and miss important pieces of information. Even if you look and listen carefully, some of the information just never seems to get to where it needs to go in your brain.

✳ You may feel overloaded if too much information comes in at one time. You may also feel this way when you can't keep up with your assignments, hand work in on time, or get things done.

✳ You may feel restless when you have to sit still or a task is boring or uninteresting to you.

✳ You may feel impatient and find that it's hard to wait. You may call out answers in class or have trouble waiting for your turn in a game. If you are impulsive, you start things before you fully understand what to do. You may rush through assignments at school without checking them afterward. This may result in many careless errors and low grades. You may feel frustrated and angry because you really knew the right answer. If this happens often, you may feel scared or anxious when you know you have a test coming up. When you feel tense, it is even harder for you to pay attention.

✳ You may find it hard to study and take tests. Even when you review the material ahead of time, the information somehow "disappears" by the time the test begins. Then you may feel forgetful and dumb.

⊛ You may feel picked on if your parents scold or nag you more than they do your brothers or sisters. You may need more reminders than other family members because your impulsive behaviors may sometimes be unsafe. Your parents care about your safety and happiness. They try to help you do the things they think are best for you, but this may sometimes feel to you like they are nagging.

⊛ You may feel unpopular. If you often say or do things before you think, other kids might not want to be with you. If you cannot wait your turn or follow the rules when you are playing games, other kids may not want to be your friend. If you are messy or can never sit still, you may be teased. All this can make you feel misunderstood.

Now for the good news!

Kids with AD/HD are just as smart as other kids. Having attention deficits does not affect your intelligence!

Kids with AD/HD also have lots of good feelings. You may feel:

Energetic   *Curious*   *Athletic*

Special   *Creative*

Artistic   *Sensitive*   *Humorous*

Attractive   *Imaginative*

Enthusiastic   *Friendly*   *Caring*

Happy

What are your feelings?

There are also some good things that come with having AD/HD:

⚙ You can use your extra energy and enthusiasm in many positive ways. You may love to run and jump, play sports, or dance. You may be very athletic, and people look up to you for those talents.

⚙ You may be a very creative person and have many good ideas. Your curiosity and imagination may help you think and do things in ways that other people may truly admire.

⚙ You may be artistic.

⚙ You may have a good sense of humor and make other people laugh.

⚙ You may be especially sensitive and caring and very aware of other people's feelings.

⚙ You may like to help people and be extremely friendly.

And, of course, kids with AD/HD are as attractive, smart, special, and as happy as anyone else.

More Good News!

Because you have had to deal with the problems of AD/HD from an early age, you have learned many things about yourself. You have the advantage of knowing your strengths and weaknesses. You know how to work hard to solve problems and accomplish your goals.

Now that you have learned more about AD/HD, the next part of the book will tell you some ways that you can put on the brakes and feel more in control of your life.

CHAPTER 6

Managing AD/HD

If you have AD/HD, you need to know that there are many things that can be done to make life easier. Treating AD/HD involves many steps and takes teamwork. You can take some of the steps to control your AD/HD by yourself. There are also many people who can help you. The following chapters will talk about how you, your parents, teachers, doctors and other professionals can work together to treat your AD/HD.

To manage your AD/HD successfully, you may need to learn new ways to interact with others. You may want to try many tools to control your behaviors and improve your schoolwork. The specialists you see will recommend many different ways to treat your AD/HD. Some specialists may **prescribe** medication to improve attention and hyperactivity. Other people may recommend that you talk with a **therapist** or work with a **resource teacher** (or **learning specialist**) in school or a **tutor** outside of school to help you with your problems or to make learning easier.

You can help by taking good care of yourself, getting plenty of exercise and choosing healthy foods to eat. You can also learn new ways to control your anger and reduce your stress levels. Teachers and tutors can help you learn new ways to become more organized and to improve your work and focus.

There is lots of good news about AD/HD now. Once you know you have it, you and your "team" can get to work to make a positive difference in your life.

CHAPTER 7

Building a Support Team

We all need people in our lives who are able to see what is special about us and give us help when things feel hard. Kids with AD/HD need support as well. It is important to know that you don't need to manage everything alone. There are many ways to get extra help.

Here are some of the ways kids with AD/HD have found support:

My family helps me out by listening to my problems and working on homework with me.

I call my grandmother in another city once a week. She is happy to hear about all the good things I've done and gives helpful advice when I have a problem.

I go to the guidance counselor at school when I need to talk about problems I'm having or how I'm feeling.

Outside of school, I go to a group with other kids. We work with a counselor who helps us understand our problems and feel good about ourselves. Sometimes the counselor also works with our families to learn new ways to help us.

I meet with a therapist to talk about my feelings and to get some new ideas for solving problems that bother me.

I meet with my teacher at school several times a month to talk, get extra help with my work, and find out if I'm missing any assignments.

My doctor helps me. She prescribes medication to help me concentrate and pay attention.

Your Support Team

When you have AD/HD, getting a little extra help can make a big difference. If you look around, you will see that there are many people who can give you some of the help you need. Depending on your needs, there may be many different people who are part of your support "team." These people might include your parents, teachers, counselor, tutors, coaches, your therapist, and your doctor.

Members of your family are a very important part of your support team. Parents can work with you to solve problems that you come across at different times. They can make homework suggestions, provide ideas for getting organized and come up with ways to help you improve your ability to focus. If something is bothering you, discussing it with a parent or other relative may give them the information they need to help you do something about it. This can also be a good way to let your parents know what they can do to be helpful to you.

Your classroom teachers work with you every day, so they have a good understanding about how you learn and how you get along with others in your class. Set up times to talk with

your teacher in private, so that together you can find ways to help you do well in your classes and do a good job with your classwork and homework.

Resource teachers (or learning specialists), tutors and coaches work with many students who have attention problems. They can provide suggestions for improving organization skills, keeping up with homework, and learning how to follow directions. Since they sometimes work with you alone or in a small group, they really get to know you and can help you figure out strategies that are designed to meet your unique needs.

School **counselors** may meet with your parents or teachers to provide them with ideas that will assist you at home or school. Some kids with AD/HD meet with a counselor to learn how to get along better with others and to make friends.

Kids with AD/HD may also meet with a therapist (a **psychologist**, counselor, or **social worker**) outside of school to better understand themselves and find ways to solve problems.

Talking with a therapist gives you an opportunity to explore the many different feelings you have. A therapist can offer suggestions to help you improve in many areas, such as learning to control your anger, making friends, getting along with your family, and finding ways to deal with teasing. Your therapist may also work with you to help you manage some of the problems that come along with your AD/HD so that you become more organized and in control. Your therapist may meet with your parents to help them understand you better and to give them suggestions for helping you at home and school.

When you talk to your therapist, you can be totally honest and say what you think. When you talk about what bothers you or what you wish could happen, your therapist will help guide you what to do next. Your therapist is on your side and ready to help make things feel a little easier.

Your medical doctor will make sure you are healthy and can also prescribe medication to help with your AD/HD symptoms if you need it. Visit your doctor regularly for check-ups and tell him how you are feeling. Be sure to report any negative side effects with your medications or other problems that you are having.

Everyone on your "team" will try to do his or her part, but you really are the most important part of this team. Your ideas, cooperation, and hard work all add up when it comes to making positive changes.

CHAPTER 8

Working Together to Manage Your Behaviors

To help you gain control over your AD/HD, it is useful for you to work with your parents and other professionals to set up a system that helps to manage your behaviors by providing structure and rewards for good behavior. By following a few simple steps, you, your parents, teachers, and other professionals can all work together to design a program to help you better manage your behaviors, allowing you to feel more in control.

Along with learning to keep your cool and handle your anger and frustration (see Chapter 10), it is important for you to work on becoming more flexible in certain situations. To learn new ways to handle yourself in difficult situations, have family meetings with your parents to brainstorm possible solutions to problems you have with others, learn how to negotiate (to have a discussion with someone so that you come to an agreement), and make decisions in ways that are acceptable to all of you. With practice, you'll be able to get along better with your family. You can use these skills with your friends, too.

Working together as a team with your parents and teachers to set up strategies will help you feel more in control. Here are some ideas for you to think about:

* Ask adults to make positive comments about your behaviors when you handle a situation well or when you are in control. When your parents say something that is helpful to you, be sure to let them know so they will also remember to do it again!

* Learn from your mistakes. Mistakes often teach us what to do differently next time. For example, when you leave your bike outside, even though the rule is to put it away, rain may cause it to rust or it might get stolen. This is a negative consequence of your behavior. Talk with your parents about situations that ended badly so that you can identify the behavior and its consequences and learn from your mistakes.

* Sometimes your parents may ignore you or get angry when you are acting badly. If you notice that your parents are ignoring you or starting to get mad, stop what you are doing and take a look at your behavior to figure out why they acted the way they did. Then talk to your parents about what they expect of you and how you can improve your behavior next time.

✳ Work with your parents and teachers to set up a system of rewards (for your positive behaviors) and consequences (for when your break the rules). This system works best when you focus on one or two behaviors at a time. Work with your parents, teachers, or counselor to understand the behaviors they are looking for. Then, you will be more likely to earn a reward. Try to find rewards that you are excited about working toward. Make sure your parents agree to what you have chosen. Having a system where you can earn tickets, tokens, or points for good behaviors works very well. Tokens or points can be taken away for negative behaviors like not meeting a goal or breaking a rule.

Let's Talk about "Time Out"

You have probably heard about "time out." Maybe you have even spent time there. You might even think of "time out" as a punishment. However, it is really meant to be a place where you can go to get yourself together and think about a situation and your own behavior. It gives you a chance to calm down so that you can then go back to what you were doing and complete it. You might even consider asking for some "time out" to gain control over your behavior and avoid getting in trouble in the first place.

As you get older, you may create your own form of "time out." Some kids use a special, quiet place to go to when they feel the need to get away or to calm down. Using music, a book or a walk may also help create a feeling of "time out" for you.

CHAPTER 9

Being a Good Friend

Now that you have learned more about AD/HD and have begun to understand yourself better, this may be a good time for you to begin working on making and keeping friends. Having more friends in your life will make you feel even better! For some kids with AD/HD, making friends can be difficult. If you always want things your way, have trouble waiting your turn, don't listen, or say and do things without thinking, other kids may not want to be your friend. You also might have trouble knowing what to say or do to be part of a group. But with some extra work, you can learn how to be a good friend.

What Makes a Good Friend?

Let's think about what makes someone a good friend. A friend:

Shares some of your interests

Shares toys, ideas, or activities

Is kind and thoughtful

Listens to what you say

Is willing to wait her turn

Find someone in your class or neighborhood with whom you feel comfortable and who is interested in some of the same things that you are. Talk to that person and make plans to get together. When you are first getting to know each other, you should plan to be together for only a little while, until you learn more about each other.

For the first few times you get together, plan on doing an activity that you both like. This could be something like working on a craft project, riding bikes, playing ball, or going to a movie. If you are going to be playing a game, work together to decide the rules of the game before you start. Make sure you don't change them once the game begins.

Be flexible and try your friend's ideas some of the time. Remember that everything should not always be done your way.

If acting impulsively (without thinking) is a problem for you, try hard to slow down and think before acting. Take a minute to look at the situation and try to think of two ways you could act instead. If a group of kids are already playing a board game and you want to join it, instead of clearing the board or sitting down and inter-rupting their game, stop and think about what you could do. Perhaps, you could ask to play in the next game or find

something else to play with until they are finished their game.

Good friends are kind and considerate. Make it a habit to say something nice about the other person each time you are together. When you are thoughtful of other people, you will be surprised by how often they are nice to you in return.

Some kids do better during planned group activities such as bowling, soccer, scouting, 4H, or other youth organizations. Other kids might do better playing at home with just one or two friends. Regardless of what works best for you, having an adult around to supervise can keep things running smoothly. If something does go wrong, the adult is there to help you.

Always feel free to discuss problems you are having with friends with your parents, counselor or therapist. With their help, you can come up with ideas and solutions. You can even practice some ways to act differently next time.

Don't forget that any friendship can have difficult moments. Sometimes the best you can do is say you are sorry or stop doing what hurt the other person. That's not easy for anyone, but it can be the best way to keep a friendship going!

CHAPTER 10

Keeping Your Cool

Getting upset or angry sometimes can be a very normal reaction. These reactions may even help you to tune in to things that are not going well and need to change. But anger can become a problem if it gets out of control and interferes with your normal day-to-day living. It is not always easy to keep your cool especially when you are frustrated, but there are some steps that you can take to help you deal with your emotions and gain better control.

Five Steps to Getting Your Emotions Under Control

You may find it helpful to work on these five steps with an adult (such as a parent or counselor) until you feel comfortable trying them on your own.

STEP ONE **Find out what makes you upset**

The most important step in controlling your emotions is identifying what situations get you upset or angry. Do you get upset when you are tired or when someone teases you? Do you have problems whenever you are with a certain person? Do you get angry when you have to rush or feel you are not being listened to? What about when you think things are unfair? Try to make a list of when you get upset and what has caused it. These situations are sometimes called your "trigger points."

STEP TWO **Avoid your "trigger points"**

Once you have made the list of what bothers you the most, the next step is to set up ways to avoid these "trigger points." That might include not playing with a certain person or moving away when you see him or her coming. It may be difficult to decide on ways to avoid your trigger points. To increase your chance for success, only work on a solution to a problem that is bothering you and making you upset when you are well rested and able to think clearly. And don't be afraid to ask for help if you need it.

If it is hard for you to find a quick solution or to avoid becoming upset or angry, the next step is to learn to recognize the signs that you are becoming angry and take steps to calm yourself down.

STEP THREE **Recognize the early signs of anger**

In order to take action against anger, you need to be aware of some of the early signs that you are getting upset. Once you learn to recognize these early warning signs, you can make changes before it is too late. Everyone has different warning signs. Here are some typical signs of anger that you may get:

*Your breathing speeds up
or you feel like you can't catch your breath.*

Your face gets red and hot.

You begin sweating.

Your heart starts beating fast.

You make fists or grit your teeth.

You start to cry.

Your voice gets louder or shaky.

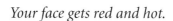

STEP FOUR **Take a Time Out**

When you have any of these early warning signals, it's a good idea to take a "time out." By moving away from the situation, you will be better able to get back into control. (See page 36 for a discussion of "time out.")

STEP FIVE **Get Back into Control**

Here are several suggestions or strategies you might try to gain better control over your emotions:

- Try counting to 10 slowly.

- Take a walk (make sure you let someone know this is what you are doing and that you are not running away!).

- Get a drink of water.

- Imagine that you are someplace else. Think of a place where you feel very comfortable, then pretend you are there.

- Practice deep breathing. (You have seen athletes do this before the big shot or the big play. Breathe in slowly to the count of 8, hold it for the count of 4, and then breathe out slowly to the count of 8. By doing this breathing 3 or 4 times, you will feel calmer.)

Other Techniques and Tools to Stay Calm

There are other ways to feel calmer, less hyperactive, and more in control. These include:

Yoga

Progressive Muscle Relaxation

Meditation

At first, you will need to practice these techniques with a parent, teacher or therapist, but soon you'll be able to use them on your own to feel calmer and more in control. Let's talk a little about each one.

Yoga

You probably have heard of yoga before but may not have known it could help kids with AD/HD. Yoga combines physical movement and postures, control of your breathing, concentration and relaxation to help you feel more in control.

But how can yoga help? To find out the answer to this question, an experiment was done with a group of 1st – 3rd grade kids with AD/HD who practiced yoga by watching a video tape, *Yoga Fitness for Kids*, with a teacher and other kids. They did this during the school day for 30 minutes, twice a week for three weeks. During the weeks when the kids were practicing yoga, the kids with AD/HD were able to focus in the classroom for the same amount of time as their classmates without AD/HD. When they stopped doing the yoga, they were still on task more than they had been before they ever started the program, but not as much as when they went to yoga sessions. Results from this study are interesting and show that yoga might indeed help kids with AD/HD pay attention better. You may want to try yoga and see if it helps you!

Progressive Muscle Relaxation

Relaxing your body with progressive muscle relaxation is a great way to help get rid of stress, calm yourself when you are angry, and quiet your mind. If you have trouble settling down during the day or falling asleep at night, try the following exercises to relax your body. By tightening and relaxing the muscles in every part of your body, you can release stress and feel calmer. You can relax any time you want by following these steps:

* Start by lying down on your back, on your bed or the floor, with your eyes closed.

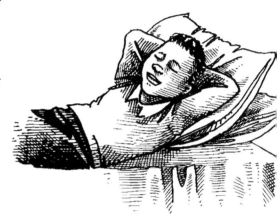

* Tighten the muscles in your toes and feet as hard as you can by curling your toes under.

* Hold this tightening while counting to 10 slowly.

* Then release and relax these muscles.

* Next tense your calves (backs of your lower legs) by pointing your toes while counting to 10.

* Relax.

* Now tighten the muscles in your legs while counting to 10.

* Relax.

* Now tighten the muscles in your stomach while counting to 10.

* Relax.

❀ Continue this tightening and relaxing with all the muscle groups in your hands, arms shoulders, neck and face.

After tightening each group of muscles, remember to hold the tightness to the count of ten and then relax the muscle group.

When you are finished with this exercise, lie quietly with your eyes closed and breathe slowly in and out for awhile. Listen to your breathing and hold on to this relaxed feeling.

Meditation

Meditation combines breathing and relaxation to help you clear your mind of all other thoughts by increasing your focus on your breathing and it can be VERY helpful especially when you are stressed or feeling out of control. Your AD/HD may make it more difficult to meditate and clear your mind, since many thoughts keep jumping in. Meditation can be difficult for many people to learn, so don't get frustrated if it takes time for you to learn it.

Meditation can be done sitting, walking, or lying down. Here is one way to meditate.

❀ Begin by sitting or lying comfortably on the floor or on a pillow.

❀ Place your hands in your lap or at your sides.

❀ Close your eyes. Breathe in and out slowly and evenly.

- Breathe in and count one.

- Breathe out to the count of two.

- Keep doing this until you reach 20.

- After you get to 20, keep breathing slowly and try to be very still. Think about things that make you happy, or just let your mind wander.

- After a few minutes, take a deep breath in and out to end the meditation.

- Next, stand up and stretch, feeling relaxed and calm.

It may take some time before you can do this exercise alone. If you are interested in meditation, you can learn how to meditate by working together with someone who teaches these techniques or you can get more ideas on meditation from the following resouces:

- *Meditation for all Kids* by Susan Kramer or her website at www.susankramer.com/ChildMeditation.html

- *Guided Meditation for Children - Journey into the Elements,* a CD by Chitra Sukhu

CHAPTER 11

Staying Focused

Staying focused is difficult for a lot of kids. It can be especially hard for kids with AD/HD. Fortunately, there are many ways you can work to improve your ability to focus. Try some of the following ideas when you are finding it hard to pay attention.

⊛ Fidgeting sometimes helps improve your focus. When you fidget, you move parts of your body, such as your fingers or toes. Try fidgeting in ways that will not bother other people but will let you move around somewhat. Some kids use a "fidget object," such as a damp sponge, a piece of clay or a squeeze ball. Make sure you let your teacher know ahead of time, so that she will know what you are doing (and why this is helpful for you).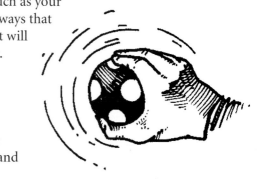

⊛ Try doodling or drawing with a pencil or marker while you are listening. This works only when you really can listen and draw at the same time.

⊛ Use different kinds of pens and pencils to make doing your work more interesting. Try using different colors also.

⊛ Keep a water bottle nearby and take sips while you are working or listening.

Having trouble focusing while you are doing your homework? Here are some more ideas for you to try:

⚙ Sometimes working with music in the background can be helpful. Different kinds of music work well for different people, so explore what is best for you.

⚙ Give yourself breaks. Work hard for a period of time (such as 15 or 20 minutes), then run around outside or do some exercise for a few minutes. Go back to work for another 15 minutes, then take another short break. You may find that you focus better during your work times this way. Use a clock or timer so that you can keep track of time.

⚙ If you have a dog or cat at home, pet it while you study. This is a nice way to get a little movement, and your pet will love you for it!

⚙ Try moving around while you study to see if it works for you. You can use a rocking chair, pedal an exercise bicycle or jump rope while you are trying to memorize something.

Exercise

Have you ever noticed how you feel calmer and more focused after P.E. class or playing sports? Getting regular exercise is important for good health, and it may help increase your attention skills. How do you usually spend your free time? If you spend a lot of time watching television or playing computer or video games, your body and brain may not be getting the exercise they really need.

What activities do you enjoy? There are lots of ways to make exercise a fun part of your life. There are plenty of activities to choose from… playing outdoors with your friends, bike riding, swimming, dancing or martial arts. They all give your body a great workout. Organized sports, such as soccer or softball, are good, too! Talk with your parents and work out a routine that will be fun and easy to follow. Together you can plan activities to make sure you get enough exercise during the busy school year.

So get out of that chair or off the couch! Move around, feel good and watch how your ability to concentrate really improves.

Playing Sports

Some kids with AD/HD enjoy playing team sports. If you are on a team, it is a good idea for you and your parents to have a talk with the coach ahead of time so he can help you play your best and avoid problems that sometimes come with being on a team. If team sports are not for you, you might consider other sports where the focus is on improving your own performance, such as swimming, diving, iceskating, or martial arts.

Getting Outdoors

Scientists have begun to study how spending time outdoors in "green space" can help improve some of the symptoms of AD/HD. Green space is any area that has trees and grass like parks and most backyards.

After spending time in these places, you may improve your focus and ability to listen to directions. Because there are so many things to do outdoors (searching for nature items, playing a game, or even reading a book), this is a good way to do something positive for yourself and have fun at the same time!

Going to Camp

Camp gives you an opportunity for you to get outdoors and be active. To make sure you have a good time at camp, use some of the same techniques that work well for you during the school year. At camp, you will be expected to follow directions, manage a schedule and keep your things organized. If you take medication during the year, be sure to discuss with your parents and doctor whether you should also be taking it at camp

CHAPTER 12

Improving Study and Organization Skills

here are many things you can do to become more in control of your life, both at home and at school. Here are some of the concerns kids with AD/HD often have:

How can I become better at following directions?

How can I become a better listener?

How can I become better organized and not lose things?

How can I keep track of all the things I need to do?

How can I manage my time well?

How can I make my work look better and neater?

How can I stop being so messy?

How should I study for tests?

These questions are answered in the following sections.

Following Directions

If it is hard for you to remember everything that your teacher tells you to do, try writing a few **key words** while the teacher is speaking. For example, your teacher is telling you about tomorrow's assignment. She says, "The work must be written in

51

cursive. It should be at least two paragraphs long. Be sure to use correct quotation marks." You can jot down a few reminder notes to look at when you get home. The notes might look like this:

1.   cursive
2.   2 paragraphs
3.   use quotation marks

Let's try another one. Your math teacher says, "Open to page 39 in your book. Do section B in class now and section C tonight for homework. Remember to use pencil and graph paper." Your notes might look like this:

MATH HOMEWORK

1.   page 39   3.   pencil
2.   section C   4.   graph paper

If it is difficult for you to write notes, try making a few quick pictures to help you remember something. Your mother says, "After dinner, feed the dog. Then clean up your desk." You can make drawings like these:

Here is another one. Your P.E. teacher says, "Bring in your sneakers and shorts for gym tomorrow." An example of some reminder drawings would be:

You may need to remind adults (parents, teachers, sports coaches) that it is hard for you to remember a lot of information when you are only hearing it. Perhaps they can write the information down for you or a classmate who writes quickly could make some notes for you. See if you can work out an arrangement with your teacher to find someone in your classes who is a fast note-taker and would be willing to help you.

Many students now use portable word processors, such as Alpha-Smarts, Quick Pads, or laptop computers at school. This is really helpful if your handwriting is hard to read or if you write slowly. Taking notes, writing reminders, and keeping track of what you need to do is much easier if you write it and store the information on your computer.

Managing Your Time

If you have trouble keeping track of time, use clocks, timers, and calendars to help. Before you start a task, take a guess at how long you think it will take to complete. Then time yourself and compare this time with your first guess. With practice, you will get better at figuring out how long things take. You can keep a record of your progress on a piece of paper or the computer.

PROJECT	AMOUNT OF TIME:	
	GUESS	ACTUAL
1. Math homework	40 minutes	20 minutes
2. Proofread book report	10 minutes	30 minutes
3. Complete spelling sentences	45 minutes	40 minutes
4. Clean backpack	2 minutes	20 minutes

Another idea is to use a timer or an alarm when you know you have only a certain amount of time to do something. This can help you to stay focused rather than get sidetracked. If you have a watch or phone with an alarm or a personal timer, you can set it to go off at the time you want to be finished, or set it a few minutes before you need to stop. These kind of watches also work well to remind you when you need to do something, such as go to the nurse's office for medicine or take your dog for her afternoon walk.

When you have lots of different things to do, it usually helps to make a list. Here are some examples of different kinds of lists that might come in handy:

THINGS TO DO TODAY

1. Get permission slip signed.
2. Study for spelling test.
3. Practice part for the play.
4. Two pages in language workbook.
5. Clean hamster cage.

Make sure to write down when an assignment or project is due. Once you have written down these due dates, you will not have to worry about remembering them in your head. Keep this information in a place where you can check it every day. Large wall calendars work well. You can use them to record the due dates. If you use a portable electronic device, such as a personal digital assistant (PDA), make sure to enter all your assignments, tests, and projects. That way it will be easier to keep track of what you need to do and the dates things are due.

When you have a large assignment, such as a research report, a big test, or a science fair project coming up, break down the assignment into smaller steps. Then write each of these steps on a separate day of the calendar so you will know what to do on each day. Some examples might be:

SUNDAY	MONDAY	TUESDAY	WEDNESDAY	THURSDAY	FRIDAY	SATURDAY
		1	2	3 READ CHAPTER 4 OF BIOGRAPHY	4	5
6	7	8 WORK ON SCIENCE FAIR PROJECT 25 MINUTES	9	10	11	12
13	14	15	16	17	18	19

Try to spread out what you have to do so that no day becomes overloaded. It may be helpful to have a parent, teacher, tutor, or counselor work with you to show you how to pace yourself and how to break big jobs down into smaller parts.

Some students like to make their running reminder lists on the computer, so they can add or take away items easily. Wipe off boards and blackboards are also easy to use, since you can erase things as they are completed, and add others that you need to remember.

Small electronic devices that fit in your pocket or backpack are great for storing lots of information: due dates, test dates, assignments, reminders, and special events. Since they are expensive and easy to lose, you may have to work out with your parents when they will be ready to let you own one.

Here is something important to remember about managing time. Things often take longer to do than we think they will, or something unexpected happens (a relative comes to visit or you get sick) that changes your original plan. So it's a good idea to build extra time into your plans. If you think something you've never done before is going to take 15 minutes, allow yourself 30 minutes. Or when planning a big assignment, plan to finish it a few days before it is due, just in case you do need some extra time toward the end.

Managing Homework

Homework assignment books can help you keep up with your work when you use them each day. Make sure to write down all of your assignments. Don't rely on your memory. If there is no assignment in a subject that day, write in "none," so it doesn't look like you forgot to write something down for that class.

Check your assignment book each day before leaving school, so you know what you will need to bring home that day. When you get home, review all that you need to do so you can

make a homework plan. A parent, homework helper, or babysitter can help you with go over what needs to be done that night.

If your school requires you to use a specific assignment book, learn how to use it at the beginning of the year. If the spaces in the book are small, decide where you will write additional homework notes and reminders to yourself. If you are allowed to choose your own assignment book, you and a parent should look for one that is well organized and gives you plenty of room to write.

You might find that it is easier to use a small hand-held electronic device, such as a PDA, to keep track of homework, tests and reminders. This is also a good place to store long-term assignments and due dates. As you complete something, you can cross it off your list. If you need to continue working on something, you can transfer it in to another date.

Some schools now have homework hotlines, so that you can call in to check on what your assignments are, or check your assignments on the school website.

If you need help understanding an assignment or just want more information on a topic, there are many websites that provide homework help to students. Some of them are run through your public library, so that is a good place to start looking. Work together with your parents and teachers to find the most useful websites when you need extra help with your homework.

Organizing Your Things

If you have a messy bedroom, school desk, locker, or backpack, talking about the problem with an adult might help you develop a better system. You may also want to give one or more of the following ideas a try:

✹ One idea some kids with AD/HD find useful is to put many shelves into their bedroom closet or on their wall. Each shelf can be marked with the name of a particular item or group of items. Using plastic baskets can also help you organize some of your things.

✹ Colors can also make organizing easier. For example, you might put all math work in a red folder and history in a green folder. Or at home, you might put underwear in a drawer with a yellow sticker, shirts in a drawer with a blue sticker, and socks in a drawer with a red sticker.

✹ Choose a specific day and time each week for cleaning out your backpack or desk. You might want to get an adult to help you with this, too.

✹ Some kids find it helpful to keep a box near the front door of the house or in a special spot in their bedroom. If you and your parents like this idea, you can use the box for schoolbooks when you come home. You can take the books out to do homework and put them back when you are finished. You can also put in anything you need for school the next day, such as your gym clothes or a permission slip for a class trip. Everything will be in one place when you are ready to leave in the morning.

✹ Make sure to pack for school the night before. This way, you will avoid rushing in the morning and you will be less likely to forget the things that you need.

Getting more organized will make your days run more smoothly and help your confidence grow.

Improving Study Habits

There are many different ways to study. Some kids with AD/HD learn better when they review or discuss material with a friend, parent, or tutor. This gives students a chance to repeat information so they will remember it better. It also allows them to ask questions if there is something they are not sure about.

Another study strategy is to underline or highlight the most important information to be studied. When you do this, you are able to focus on only the material you need to know, instead of paying attention to the extra, less important information.

Some students study while using a tape recorder, reading aloud the most important points from notes or the book. They later listen to the recorded notes over and over. This works well for kids who need to hear things several times in order to really learn them. Also, when you speak into the tape recorder, you are saying the information in a way that you can understand it.

Students who get restless easily sometimes find that moving around while they study is helpful. This helps get rid of some of your extra energy, which may then make it easier for you to concentrate. Try walking as you read or pedal an exercise bicycle, if there is one in your house. Another idea is to exercise before you begin your studying. This may help you feel more relaxed when you get started.

If your teacher gives you a study guide, make sure to use it when you prepare for a test because it is a good way to know what your teacher considers important. You can also make up your own study guide or work together with a classmate and make one together.

Kids who have trouble concentrating sometimes need to find a quiet study place that has very few distractions. Think of a place where you can focus best and try to study there.

When you concentrate hard, you may need to take regular short breaks so that you don't start to feel sleepy or bored. Walk around, play a short game of catch, or go get a healthy snack. The change and movement will help you get back to work with improved focus.

Try studying in different places or positions. Some kids like listening to music when they study. Try different techniques for studying, even those you had never considered. The purpose of these efforts is to help you figure out the ways that work best for you. Some kids have a few ways that they study best. Other kids find that one way or one place works best. Get to know what works for you, and experiment with some new ways every once in awhile. As you get older, you may discover new techniques as well.

Improving Schoolwork

Some kids find it useful to sit near the front of the classroom in order to decrease distractions.

Some teachers may help kids focus on their work by giving them a pre-arranged secret signal to remind them to get back on track. Some examples include the teacher tapping her desk or holding a special pencil. (If the teacher agrees to help you stay on track in this way, you and your teacher can come up with your own signal.)

Before you start your work, it is a good idea to read all the directions at least two times. This way, you will make sure to do the right thing from the start.

It is important that you check over your classwork and homework. You want your teachers to see how much you really know, so show them work without careless errors.

Doing work on the computer makes it look better, and it is much easier to correct any mistakes. Check in with your teacher to see which work you are allowed to do this way. Also remember to ALWAYS back up your work on the computer so you don't lose it.

Improving Proofreading

Proofreading means looking over your work for any mistakes. Look for mistakes in spelling, punctuation, and capitalization. Although proofreading your work doesn't always seem like much fun, it is the best way to find mistakes and then you'll turn in work that makes you feel proud.

Check to see if all your sentences are complete and make sense. Read out loud what you wrote as a way of making sure that the sentences say what you meant.

Read your paper from the bottom to the top. This may help you spot your spelling and punctuation errors more easily.

Make a game of it. See how many mistakes you can find in five minutes. Exchange papers with a friend and look for errors in each other's work.

Use the computer for longer homework assignments. You will find it easier to spot mistakes.

Use the **spell-check** program on your computer. You can also buy a small portable spell-check device that you can use in school.

Organizing Your Ideas

Some kids with ADD or ADHD have lots of good ideas but find it hard to organize their thoughts into writing. Using graphic organizers, such as webs or outlines, is a good way to set up your ideas before you start writing. You write your ideas down and organize them into categories, so when you begin to write, you have an order to follow. Some graphic organizers have different sections for you to fill in with your ideas. Then, when you are getting ready to write your assignment, you can use the organizer as your guide. Your teacher may give you

some examples of graphic organizers to complete so that you get practice using them. There is also software for graphic organizers on the computer, which can be very helpful.

Improving Test Results

Study for each test over a period of many days. This makes it easier to review all the material and you will feel less nervous. As you begin a test, take a deep breath and remind yourself that you are prepared!

Don't pick up that pencil to start the test until you have read all of the directions at least two times. During the test, check the clock a few times (or bring a watch) so that you make sure you are using your time well.

Keep a few pieces of clean paper on your desk when you take a test. If you find it hard to remember information, use the blank paper to jot down everything that does come into your head about the subject. This is a trick that will help you recall the material you have studied.

When you take an essay test, write notes on the paper, reminding yourself what you want to be sure to include in your answer. You can also write a quick outline or web with your ideas, so that you can follow it when you write your essay. Once you begin the essay, you can always look back and not worry about forgetting an important point.

Always check over a test paper completely before you hand it in. Wait a few minutes and then check it again.

When your graded test is returned, take some time to review it. See what you did well and what you need to improve next time. Talk it over with a parent, teacher, or tutor who might be able to help you figure out how to better prepare the next time you have a test.

CHAPTER 13

Taking Care of Yourself

Taking good care of yourself includes getting enough sleep, eating healthy foods, staying safe and feeling good about yourself. This may mean a little extra work, but it will be worth it.

Getting Enough Sleep

Getting enough sleep helps you feel more alert and focused the next day. Sometimes kids with AD/HD have trouble falling asleep or getting enough sleep at night. This can make them **irritable** and less attentive the next day. If you have difficulty falling asleep, here are some tips that might help you:

⊛ Listen to quiet music.

⊛ Try the progressive relaxation or meditation techniques described on pages 44–46.

⊛ Make sure your room is dark so you are not distracted by things.

⊛ Don't play video games or do homework right before getting into bed.

⊛ Take a relaxing bath in the evening.

⊛ Pack your bookbag and set out your clothes before you go to sleep so you don't have to worry about them.

✳ Get enough exercise during the day, but not right before bedtime. Also, no rough or exciting play right before bedtime. Getting too excited might make it difficult to settle down.

✳ Have a small snack earlier in the evening, so you won't be hungry when you're trying to fall asleep. It is important to be careful what you eat: A snack that has lots of sugar or caffeine, like cola or chocolate, may keep you awake.

If you still have problems falling asleep after trying some of these ideas, you and your parents might want to talk to your doctor about it.

Eating Right

Eating a balanced diet helps you grow and have enough energy to learn and play. Some kids who take medication for their AD/HD might have less of an appetite during the day. If this happens to you, it is important to make sure that you choose foods that will provide good nutrition (not unhealthy foods like sugary or fatty junk food). You need to eat these healthful foods throughout the day to keep up your energy and to help you grow. This might mean that you eat a healthy breakfast (like fruit, waffles, yogurt, cereal, or toast) and a smaller lunch (half a sandwich, a chicken leg with carrot sticks, or yogurt and fruit) with a larger afternoon snack (pasta, a hamburger, or soup and crackers) or an early dinner when your appetite returns.

These foods are only suggestions. Your doctor or a nutritionist can give you more ideas and answer your questions. It is important that you work together with your parents so that they can have your favorite healthy foods that are low in sugar, caffeine, and fat in the house. Doctors have also found that it is important that kids with AD/HD avoid foods that have too many artificial ingredients, like food colorings and preservatives, that have been found to make hyperactive behaviors worse.

Staying Safe

When kids with AD/HD act impulsively or don't take the time to think about what they are doing, they may have more accidents or get into trouble more often. To avoid many of these problems it helps to:

⊛ Be with friends who know how to play safely.

⊛ Review safety rules with your parents.

⊛ Play where an adult is nearby to supervise.

⊛ Make believe your parent or teacher is standing right next to you. What would he or she tell you to do?

Feeling Good about Yourself

If you have a difficult day, or your parents complain about your behavior or say that you never listen to their directions, it would be easy to start feeling badly about yourself. At these times, it is important to remind yourself that you do have lots to be proud of and that you are good at a lot of things. Try to remember your many good qualities. Sometimes, making a list (either in your head or on paper) of nice things that have happened can improve the way you feel.

Things I'm GOOD at

NICE Things that Have Happened to Me

CHAPTER 14

Learning about Medications for AD/HD

For some kids with AD/HD, the doctor may prescribe a **stimulant medication** (also called **stimulants**) to help with their attention problems. Stimulants are drugs that are used to increase focus and attention. Stimulants can also reduce extra moving around or hyperactivity by "turning on the brakes" in the brain.

Stimulants are used to improve the way the brain works. They are not given because someone is sick, like other medicines.

Here are some of the things that kids have said about taking medication to treat their AD/HD:

It helps me get my work done.

It's like glue. Before, my thoughts were all in pieces. The medicine stuck them all together.

It's my memory and concentration pill.

It helps me not climb the walls or get into trouble.

Before, my brain was cloudy, but now it's all cleared up.

I feel more organized.

It helps me pay better attention.

Thirty minutes after I take my medicine, the AD/HD just packs up and moves out.

It helps me think one thought at a time.

After I take my medication, I'm not so hyper and don't feel like I need to get out of my seat.

It is my band-aid, just like a band-aid for my brain.

It helps me calm down.

It lets me show how smart I am.

65

What You Need to Know

If your doctor has prescribed medicine for your AD/HD, it is important that you learn as much as you can about it, including its name, what it looks like, and the **dose** (amount) you are suppose to take each time. This is all very important information.

You should never take a medicine when you don't know what it is. Only take medicine from someone who is allowed to give it to you, such as your parent, babysitter, or the school nurse. You should not take anyone else's medication, ever. You should also never share your medicine with anyone else, even if they have the same problems paying attention that you have.

Medication Is Only One Part of AD/HD Treatment

Medications can be very helpful if you have AD/HD. But the medication can't do everything. If you have problems with schoolwork, organization, or getting along with others, you still need to learn ways to improve. Members of your "team" are there to help you. For example, medication may help you improve your concentration, but to do better in school, you may need to spend extra time with your teacher or tutor to learn better study skills. You still need to put in the time studying and do all of your assignments, but you may find that schoolwork will go more smoothly once you are more organized and better focused.

The Right Medication for You

AD/HD affects your life. All day. Every day. While some kids may only need medication during the school day, others may need medication later in the day for homework, after-school activities, and getting along at home.

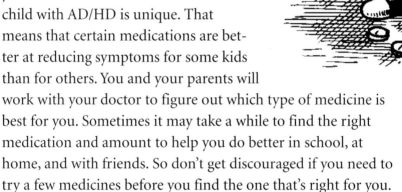

Today, there are many medications to treat AD/HD. With so many medications available, you, your parents, and your doctor have lots of choices. Each child with AD/HD is unique. That means that certain medications are better at reducing symptoms for some kids than for others. You and your parents will work with your doctor to figure out which type of medicine is best for you. Sometimes it may take a while to find the right medication and amount to help you do better in school, at home, and with friends. So don't get discouraged if you need to try a few medicines before you find the one that's right for you.

Medications to Treat AD/HD

Stimulants are the most common medications used to treat AD/HD. Stimulants are medicines that increase attention and concentration by changing the levels of the neurotransmitters in the brain and making the brain's receptors work more efficiently (See Chapter 4 for a review of what's going on in your brain). This makes focusing and learning easier. Stimulants can also decrease impulsivity and help you manage your own behavior by being able to follow the rules and doing what you know is right. Stimulants have been used to treat AD/HD for a long time. Over the years, many hundreds of **research studies** have been done to prove that these stimulant medications to treat AD/HD are safe when used correctly.

Medications prescribed for treating AD/HD come in different forms that last for different lengths of time. We call these *short-, intermediate-, and long-acting* medications depending on how long a pill works. Your doctor and your parents, with input from you and your teachers, will decide which medicine is right for you, depending on how long you need it to work.

Short-acting Medications

These medications usually start working about 20 minutes after you take them, and last about 4 hours. If these pills are taken before school or early in the morning, they will usually wear off by lunch. Your doctor might then recommend another pill at lunchtime at school. A third dose (amount) of medication is sometimes needed to help attention during homework and other after-school activities. The most commonly used brand of the short-acting medicines are Ritalin, Dexedrine, and Adderall. These are all stimulants.

Intermediate-acting Medications

These pills last a little longer (up to 6 hours) and often allow kids to get through the entire school day by taking only one pill in the morning. If that pill wears off after school, a *short-acting* pill may be needed for activities or homework. The intermediate-acting forms of these medications are also stimulants. They are Ritalin SR, Metadate CD, and Focalin.

Long-acting Medications

The effects of long-acting medications usually last for 10 to 12 hours. With each of these medicines, only one pill or patch is needed in the morning, and its effects usually last into the evening. Long-acting stimulant pills used to treat AD/HD are named Concerta, Focalin XR, Vyvanse, and Adderall XR. There is also a newer way to give a stimulant for AD/HD by using a skin patch. This patch is called Daytrana. Once the patch is stuck on your skin, it gives you a stimulant medicine for AD/HD through your skin. This patch is usually worn for 9 hours, but the medicine's effect lasts for about 12 hours.

There are also long-acting medications that are **non-stimulants** (not stimulants). These non-stimulants act a little bit differently in the brain, but still help control AD/HD through-out the day. The one most commonly used is called Strattera.

Each year new medications are being made. Some work better and last longer. AD/HD cannot be cured, but it can be controlled with lots of help. Medication can be a part of that help. Over time, your AD/HD may improve, but it is important to continue to work with your doctor so that you receive the best treatment to keep your symptoms under good control.

Side Effects

Sometimes medicines may make people feel a certain way when they are taken. These problems are known as **side effects**. Some of the medicines commonly used to treat AD/HD may make you feel less hungry. This doesn't happen to everyone, but if it does happen to you, it is important that you not lose weight. Eat a good breakfast, and try to eat something at lunchtime. You can also make up for lost calories by eating nutritious snacks in the afternoon and before you go to bed at night.

A few kids complain about a slight stomachache after they take the medicine. Be sure to tell your parents, doctor, or teacher if you have that problem. Eating some crackers or drinking a glass of water will usually make the feeling go away. You can also try drinking a full glass of water when taking the pill, instead of just a sip. That may prevent the stomachache from happening in the first place.

You should avoid citrus drinks or fruits (orange, grapefruit, lemon, or lime) when you take some stimulant medicines because they can reduce the effectiveness of the medicine. You can take most of the stimulant medications before or after you eat without it making a difference.

Working Together with Your Doctor

Remember to tell your parents and doctor how the medicine you take makes you feel so that they can help you. Visit your doctor and have a check-up regularly while you are taking your medicine. She or he can check your height, weight, and **blood pressure**, and do blood tests, if needed, to make sure you are healthy and growing.

Your doctor is the person in charge of your medicine. By following your progress closely, your doctor will be able to decide how much medicine you need and when you should take it. Sometimes doctors adjust the dose or change the medication until the best one for you can be found. Be sure to let your doctor know how the medicine works for you. Describe any changes you have noticed. Make sure all of your opinions and questions are heard and answered.

AFTERWORD
To Boys and Girls with ADD or ADHD

You have taken a big step by reading this book and learning what attention deficit disorders are all about. We hope you now know more about taking control of your life and about how to put on the brakes.

Now you can use this knowledge to make many positive changes in your life. Remember that having ADD or ADHD will not stop you from doing the things you want to do. With hard work and believing in yourself, you can succeed.

Read any sections of this book when you need it. With each reading, you will get more ideas to make things in your life easier and more positive. Remember, although the suggestions in this book may seem like extra work, they are worth trying in order to make things better at home and at school.

Encourage the important people in your life (such as family members, teachers, friends, and classmates) to read this book and to learn more about AD/HD and you. Don't be afraid to ask for help when you need it. There are many people who are willing to help you.

Talk to your parents, teachers, doctor and therapist to learn more about yourself. Work with them as you try the ideas in this book. Together you may also come up with other suggestions. You really can change and make improvements. Be creative! See what works for you and use it!

Your AD/HD is just one part of you. Try hard to manage it, and you will have plenty of energy left over to enjoy the many other parts of life as well.

Best wishes,
Patricia O. Quinn, M.D.
Judith M. Stern, M.A.

GLOSSARY

A

Adaptable. Able to fit into many different situations

Attention Deficit Disorder (ADD). A set of problems that includes difficulty paying attention and focusing. It also includes increased distractibility.

Attention Deficit Hyperactivity Disorder (AD/HD). A condition in a person of average or above-average intelligence that includes symptoms such as short attention span, distractibility, impulsivity, and/or hyperactivity.

B

Blood Pressure. The pressure of the blood against the inner walls of the blood vessels. It can be measured by a cuff placed around the upper arm.

Brain. The major organ of the nervous system. It controls all mental and physical activities.

Brain Stem. A part of the brain that controls automatic functions such as breathing, heart rate, and blood pressure.

C

Cerebellum. A part of the brain that controls the movements of the muscles, helps with balance, and controls attention.

Cerebral Cortex. The outermost layer of the brain. Its networks are essential to higher thinking activities such as memory and organizing information. It makes up 40% of total brain weight.

Concentrate. To pay attention

Conscious. A state of being awake and aware of what is going on around you.

Counselor. A professional who works with kids or adults to help them understand feelings and solve their problems. Counselors may work in schools or have offices in other places.

D

Depression. Feeling sad and hopeless for a long time.

Diagnosis. Identification and description of a condition or problem.

Disorganization. Difficulty keeping track of materials and/or time.

Distractibility. Trouble staying focused on just one thing.

Dose. The correct amount of medicine a person needs to take at one time for the medicine to work properly.

Due Date. The date on which an assignment or project needs to be handed in.

E

Evaluation. Testing to determine how you are doing in school, how you are feeling, or to find out if you have a problem in one or more areas.

H

Hyperactivity. Excessive body movements that are usually without a purpose and greater than normally seen at a certain age.

I

Impulsivity. Acting or speaking without thinking.

Inherited. Passed down from generation to generation.

Inhibit. To hold back.

Intelligence. The ability to learn.

Irritable. Overly sensitive or in a bad mood.

K

Key Words. The most important words, such as a few words you would use to identify an assignment or remind yourself to do something.

L

Learning Disabilities. Significant difficulties in learning to read, write, or do mathematics that cause problems in school achievement.

Learning Specialist. A teacher who has special training in working with students who have learning difficulties.

M

Medication. Substances used to treat illnesses or to improve functioning of the body or brain.

N

Neurologist. A medical doctor who is a specialist in the way the nervous system works. The nervous system of the body is made up of the brain, spinal cord, and nerves.

Neuron. A single brain cell.

Neurotransmitters. Chemical substances produced by brain cells (neurons) that act as messengers. They cross the space (synapse) between cells and carry information to other brain cells.

Non-stimulant Medication. Medication used to treat AD/HD that acts differently than the stimulants on the chemicals in the brain but still improves attention and focus.

O

Organized. Being able to put things in their correct order or place.

P

Pediatrician. A medical doctor who is a specialist in the health of kids and adolescents.

Prearranged. Planned ahead.

Prescribe. To write directions for the preparation and use of a medicine.

Professional. A person with special training and a university degree or license in a particular area.

Proofreading. Checking over written work for errors in spelling, punctuation, capitalization, and grammar.

Psychiatrist. A medical doctor who specializes in helping people who are having difficulties with their feelings or behaviors. This doctor can also prescribe medication.

Psychologist. A doctor who talks with people to help them understand their thoughts, feelings, and behaviors. Some psychologists also do testing to learn more about people so they can help them.

Q

Questionnaire. A form containing questions that people answer to provide information.

R

Receptors. Sites on a brain cell (neuron) that receive messages in the form of neurotransmitters from other brain cells.

Relay System. A system in the subcortex of the brain that coordinates information coming in from the brain stem and sends it to the cerebral cortex and other parts of the brain.

Resource Teacher. A special education teacher who works with kids individually or in small groups. Some schools call them Learning Specialists.

Research Studies. Experiments conducted by scientists to learn about what causes certain conditions and what works best to make these conditions better.

S

Scans. Special pictures taken of the brain.

Side Effects. Uncomfortable reactions that are sometimes caused by medicine.

Social Worker. A professional who works with kids and their families to help them solve their problems.

Spansule. A type of pill that delivers medication over a longer period of time.

Spell-check. A program for the computer or small, hand-held machine that is used to find and correct spelling mistakes.

Stimulant Medication. Drugs that increase attention and focus. Stimulants commonly used to treat AD/HD: Ritalin, Dexedrine, Concerta, Daytrana, Focalin, Adderall, Metadate, and Vyvanse.

Stressful. Something that makes a person feel tense or uncomfortable

Subcortex. The area of the brain below and surrounded by the cerebral cortex.

Synapse. An extremely small space between two brain cells (neurons) that can be seen only with a microscope. Neurons send messages to each other across synapses.

T

Theories. Explanations that have not yet been proved to be true.

Therapist. A professional who works with kids or adults to solve problems, understand feelings, or change behavior. A therapist can be a psychologist, counselor, social worker, or psychiatrist.

Therapy. Talking with a specialist to understand problems and learn how to deal with them.

Transporter System. A system of proteins in the brain that carry chemicals across the cell membranes. When a brain cell (neuron) releases a neurotransmitter (messenger) into a synapse (space), the transporter system is responsible for taking the neurotransmitter back into the cell that released it.

Tutor. A person who works with kids outside of class to help them learn to do better in school. A tutor may help with a particular subject area, such as math, or learning in general. Tutors can also help kids improve their organization and study skills.

RESOURCES
Books for Kids

TO LEARN MORE ABOUT AD/HD

Learning to Slow Down and Pay Attention, Third Edition
  by Kathleen Nadeau and Ellen Dixon (Magination Press)

The Survival Guide for Kids with ADD or AD/HD
  by John Taylor (Free Spirit Press)

*Distant Drums, Different Drummers: A Guide for Young People With
  AD/HD* by Barbara Ingersoll (Cape Publications)

Help Is on the Way: A Child's Book About ADD
  by Jane Annunziata and Marc Nemiroff (Magination Press)

Adolescents and ADD: Gaining the Advantage
  by Patricia Quinn (Magination Press)

TO READ ABOUT KIDS WITH AD/HD

Phoebe Flower's Adventures by Barbara Roberts (Advantage Books)
  That's What Kids Are For
  Phoebe's Lost Treasure
  Phoebe's Best Best Friend
  Phoebe's Tree House Secrets

Sparky's Excellent Misadventures: My ADD Journal, By Me (Sparky)
  by Phyllis Carpenter and Marti Ford (Magination Press)

*Otto Learns About His Medicine: A Story About Medication
  for Children With ADHD, Third Edition* by Matthew Galvin
  (Magination Press)

Joey Pigza Swallowed a Key by Jack Gantos (HarperTrophy)

*Jumpin' Johnny Get Back to Work! A Child's Guide to
  ADHD/Hyperactivity* Michael Gordon (GSI Publications)

Ethan Has Too Much Energy: An Emotional Literacy Book
  by Lawrence Shapiro (Boulden Publishing)

TO HELP YOU DO BETTER IN SCHOOL

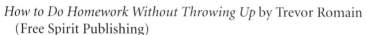

Annie's Plan: Taking Charge of Schoolwork and Homework by Jeanne Kraus (Magination Press)

Get Organized without Losing It by Janet Fox (Free Spirit Publishing)

How to Be School Smart: Super Study Skills, Revised Edition by Elizabeth James and Carol Barkin (Beech Tree Books)

How to Do Homework Without Throwing Up by Trevor Romain (Free Spirit Publishing)

Many Ways to Learn: Young People's Guide to Learning Disabilities by Judith Stern and Uzi Ben-Ami (Magination Press)

The Survival Guide for Kids With LD (Learning Differences) (Revised and Updated) by Rhonda Cummings and Gary Fisher (Free Spirit Publishing)

TO HELP WITH FEELINGS AND BEHAVIORS

The Behavior Survival Guide for Kids: How to Make Good Choices and Stay Out of Trouble by Thomas McIntyre (Free Spirit)

What to Do Guides for Kids by Dawn Huebner (Magination Press)
  What to Do When You Worry Too Much:
    A Kid's Guide to Overcoming Anxiety
  What to Do When You Grumble Too Much:
    A Kid's Guide to Overcoming Negativity
  What to Do When Your Temper Flares:
    A Kid's Guide to Overcoming Problems with Anger
  What to Do When You Dread Your Bed:
    A Kid's Guide to Overcoming Problems with Sleep

TO HAVE FUN LEANING ABOUT AD/HD — GAMES AND ACTIVITIES

50 Activities and Games for Kids with ADD by Patricia Quinn and Judith Stern (Magination Press)

The "Putting on the Brakes" Activity Book for Young People with ADHD by Patricia Quinn and Judith Stern (Magination Press)

RESOURCES FOR YOGA AND MEDITATION

Yoga Fitness for Kids Ages 7-12 (VHS) by Leah Kalish (Living Arts/Giam)

Meditation for All Kids by Susan Kramer (Susan Kramer.com Publishing)

Guided Meditation for Children: Journey into the Elements CD by Chitra Sukhu (New Age Kids)

Books for Parents

School Strategies for ADD Teens: Guidelines for Schools, Parents, and Students: Grades 6-12 by Kathleen Nadeau, Ellen Dixon, and Susan Biggs (Advantage Books)

Parenting Children With ADHD: 10 Lessons That Medicine Cannot Teach by Vincent J. Monastra, PhD (APA Books)

Taking Charge of ADHD, Revised Edition: The Complete, Authoritative Guide for Parents by Russell Barkley (Guilford Press)

The ADHD Book of Lists: A Practical Guide for Helping Children and Teens with Attention Deficit Disorders by Sandra Rief (Jossey-Bass)

ADHD: A Complete and Authoritative Guide by Michael I. Reiff with Sherill Tippins (American Academy of Pediatrics)

Software for Graphic Organizers

Kidspiration® (grades K-5) by Inspiration Software, Inc. "Kidspiration® provides a way for students to build visual diagrams to represent thoughts and organize information."*

Draft:Builder (grades 3-12) by Don Johnston Inc. "Draft:Builder helps develop an approach to planning, organizing and draft-writing. It breaks the writing process into small, manageable chunks so that students stay on task and develop effective writing habits."

Audio Books

Recordings for the Blind and Dyslexic
  phone: (866) 732-3585
  www.rfbd.org

For a list of libraries carrying audio books, you and your parents
should visit the Library of Congress online at: www.loc.gov/nls

Organizational Materials

Organizational Tools for Students in Grades 3-12
  This catalog of useful materials for students contains items such as
  structured assignment notebooks and calendars.
  To order, contact:
      Success by Design Inc.
      3741 Linden Avenue, SE, Wyoming, MI 49548
      phone: (800) 327-0057
      www.successbydesign.com

Organizations Focusing on AD/HD

Attention Deficit Disorder Association (ADDA)
  15000 Commerce Parkway, Suite C, Mount Laurel, NJ 08054
  phone: (858) 439-9099
  www.add.org

Children and Adults with Attention Deficit Disorder (CHADD)
  8181 Professional Place, Suite 150, Landover, MD 20785
  phone: (800) 233-4050
  www.chadd.org

National Center for Girls and Women with AD/HD
  3268 Arcadia Place, NW, Washington, DC 20015
  phone: (888) 238-8588
  www.ncgiadd.org